Swans Island Buoys and Other Lines

Swans Island Buoys and Other Lines

Donald Junkins

iUniverse, Inc.
New York   Bloomington

Swans Island Buoys and Other Lines

The views expressed in this work are solely those of the author and do not necessarily reflect the views of the publisher, and the publisher hereby disclaims any responsibility for them.

iUniverse books may be ordered through booksellers or by contacting:

iUniverse
1663 Liberty Drive
Bloomington, IN 47403
www.iuniverse.com
1-800-Authors (1-800-288-4677)

Because of the dynamic nature of the Internet, any Web addresses or links contained in this book may have changed since publication and may no longer be valid.

ISBN: 978-1-4502-4431-2 (sc)
ISBN: 978-1-4502-4433-6 (dj)
ISBN: 978-1-4502-4432-9 (ebk)

Printed in the United States of America

iUniverse rev. date: 11/1/2010

Books by Donald Junkins

Poems:
The Sunfish and the Partridge
The Graves of Scotland Parish
Walden, 100 Years after Thoreau
and sandpipers she said
The Agamenticus Poems
The Uncle Harry Poems
Crossing by Ferry
Playing for Keeps
Journey to the Corrida
Late at Night in the Rowboat

Anthology:
The Contemporary World Poets

Fiction:
Half Hitch

Translations:
Euripides' *Andromache*
The Tagore Reader (with Amiya Chakravarty)

Some of these poems have appeared previously in *The New Yorker, The Virginia Quarterly Review, North Dakota Quarterly, The Poetry Miscellany, Contemporary New England Poetry*, Vol. I and II, *Field, A Year in Poetry*, and later appeared also in book form in the author's *Crossing by Ferry, The Uncle Harry Poems, Playing for Keeps*, and *Late at Night in the Rowboat*.

Contents

For Yunwei

Clyde Torrey and the author picking Clyde's vegetables in the mid-seventies

I

"*On this fine August Day with the sun shining on the fine Swans Island Terrain that we of this place love so well; I find pleasure piled up on pleasure placing in My New neighbors and Friends hands this fine book* [Biography of an Island]. . . . *I am now Retired and living on the old farm; now the Morison Tent grounds address Atlantic Me.*"

[signed] *Capt. Clyde M. Torrey Retired* [1970]

"Approaches To Blue Hill Bay":
Chart No. 13313

Late June, walking the deer runs
to Goose Pond after supper
summer begins. Sidestepping
stormblown poplars,
dry-wading the slash from the pulpers' camps
ten years ago, keeping the imaginary
straight line from Duck Island Light to the north side
of Goose Pond Mountain in our minds' eyes; poking
our fish poles through young hackmatack
straight-arms, trying to keep from snagging
the green fur, the purple stars on the schooldesk landscape
of the nautical chart.

                         Yellow, blue.
The island woods are yellow. The evening sun
sprays through from the other side of the evergreens.
Woodcolors, our first grade pegs
arranging. We push for the first view
of the marsh-edged shore, spruce stumpsticks
edging deep water trout
neverminding the cold. We know where we are:
a mile straight in on the yellow.
We lose our way. My son climbs a blue spruce
to see where we've been: the two Sisters,
Long Island Plantation. On the left, the Baptist
church in Atlantic. We head into the sun.

Late June, walking the deer runs
to Goose Pond after supper
summer begins suddenly. We can hear
the creeing of gulls. Beyond the trees
they are landing, taking off, landing.
Saltwhite. Freshblue. It is all
pre-arranged. In a minute now
we will see the pond. Nothing has changed.

After Catching Mackerel Off Kent's Wharf

Twenty years ago Richard competed
here with the Fisherman's Co-op two wharves down
in Burnt Coat Harbor, before he moved his float
to the Mackerel Cove side of the Carrying Place.
Now pigeons coo beneath the pressure-treated
two-by-eights, and the tenders of lobster boats
rock on their plastic buoys in the late morning
breeze. The harbor is ruffled clean blue lace
as the *Annette Marie* sidles to unload
and weigh the morning's haul. The wharf's black
Labrador retriever barks for his cracker
treat, and Normie Burns obliges, goading
him for fun. This September day
is white and blue with old island ways.

Lines Begun Near The Shore In A High Wind

The low roof pot swings
empty over the dark deck; two blue
flags snap-flutter on grommet rings
down the driftwood mast. "Who

are you dear?" my mother asked
last summer, eating her apple, her wig
awry under the sweeping gull's eye, basking
sweater-cozy in the sun. I was rigging

the extension ladder to stain the topmost
cedar shakes. "You mean I *bore*
you?"—and struck the driftwood railing post
laughing, nibbling her apple core

to the seeds. She dozed in the August
heat. I dabbed and brushed the dark
oil in as the breeze wavered in cooling gusts
off the water. In her sleep she mumbled "Hark,

hark." Later she said, "You mustn't mind me, dear,
but where have I been all these years?"
Now the island weather has changed again.
The blue flags drape, and the fog is rolling in.

The Night Island Wind

A big-eared mouse appears
and disappears behind the corner
boot, hearing

no footfall, no heavy-handed
log topping the birch-sogged
flames. Dead

soot crisps and drops into the fall's
first fireplace glow. All
summer I followed

her tracks with an owner's scorn
for untidy guests horning
in. Now shorn

of the easy confidence that comes
lying alone in the August sun,
pastor John,

I am undone in my own house.
I hear the high tide roar as the mouse
carefully browses

in the tinkling pans. Without wit
I brought Joan the deadly news at lunch, the tidbit
that hurts,

and headed out on the ferry's leisurely run
to the oiled deck cold with beach stones,
pine cones

piled for the autumn fire. Wee

beastie, Burns called you and me,
listen: the sea

roars exactly as the half-moon
rises over the yodel of the gone
summer loon.

Deep June Onshore, Opening Up

The wind rushes the poplars, and the wild rose
ruffles by the rotting deck. I cannot see
Ram Island for the larch arms now between me
and old news. Whose death tolls

off Sunken Money Ledge? I have cut
a hundred branches to keep the lower
view. Earlier, two kayaks and their paddlers
gleamed from Red Point to the Sister Islands' hut.

Here my deck chair frays. The railing-mast
from the Muscongus Bay sloop floats
between deck posts, punky: my daughter's seven coats
of yellowed varnish peels. The past

is something else again. When I was a child
I found a Collier's magazine in a gold mine camp
above Lynn Bay, Alaska, Eddie Cantor
ogling on the cover, asking calmly wild-eyed,

"Will America ever be rich again?" Last night
at dusk I untied the nylon knot on the bleached-pole
nail and raised the Big Dipper toward the black hole
in the sky. Now in the morning light

the blue flag flutters against the spruce dark green
toward the open sea. Off in the woods a mourning dove
knits and pearls. I cannot measure the silence of this cove
as the noon tide comes in. Overhead a single gull careens.

You Came Up From The Tide Pool

with a pocketful of periwinkles
that Sunday morning in August
before the wind shifted east
and the blown petrels laced the darkening
waves: sprinkles first,

then a higher sea watermarking
the seawall beach, then larch arms
drunken across the window sky. At night
the waning moon lighted
the punky walkway from the car,

and the tentative deer
crossed silently toward the shore.

A White Sailboat In Late July

slides soundlessly behind the west Sister point
as the grasshopper touches down and sailflutters up
and settles on our deck. His ladyfinger flaps
grind his own ax in the summer sun:

relax. I watch his tucked wings mimic
the rotting bleached-cracked spruce
until he jumps the southwest breeze. Summer arithmetic
in yellow blotches scars the blueberry sea.

Markings

Here in a rift of the island ledge
I watch the morning shore. Voices
from Red Point drift down, my children's
play. It is late July, the tide
is coming in. Effortlessly, a gull
rises, drops a hermit crab on a rock

and eats. White wings mark the rock
among a million stones marked off by ledge:
a seawall beach of stones, the color of gulls'
eggs, basking. I cannot sound the voices
in those stones. I count sails and tides,
I count the days. I count the ways my children

grow here by the shore before their own children
come and go. My sons bounce rocks
off bigger rocks into the sea—the tides
will bring them back more round (even the ledges
wear away). A schooner tacks, voices
carry. Three jibs luff like flailing gulls.

Last week an eagle flew by, harassed by gulls.
We were eating supper. One of the children
shouted, "The eagle!" We jumped up, our voices
marking its flight across the beach rocks,
over the spruces behind Red Point ledge—
then it was gone like a speck into the tide.

I watch the rockweed weaving in the tide.
A southwest breeze blows up, two gulls
take off. The gong off Sunken Money Ledge
sounds its iron sound, unlike my children
edging down the shore: they jump from rock
to ledge to rock, calling. Their voices

sound across the beach like porpoise voices
sounding in the blue. They stare at the tide-
line moving over the darkening rocks.
They keep track of their day: gulls,
boats, herons, seals—the way that children
do. They wave, crossing behind my ledge.

Summer children mark their island ways. The tide
marks every rock along the beach. Soon the nearby gulls
will watch from this ledge: I hear them now above my voice.

Westward Of Swans Island

off the Hockamock Head three miles:
Sand Cove.
We dove
from our anchored sloop, freestyle-

ing over the shallow ground shells
finer then
sand, ran
the beach until our footprints fell

into the tide. The August sun
bore down.
Rolling brown
toggle buoys over the tons

of shell grains baking in the curve
of shore,
we bore
down too. The hard foam swerved,

jumped hand to hand, touching each
other, island
to island.
We sailed to Marshall Island on a close reach

and played in the summer ways. We
even found
high aground
a bottle with a letter, tossed into the sea

four months before off the Tuckernuck Shoals
buoy, mapped
and capped
with wax in Nantucket Sound by souls

crossing in the spring on the underside of
Massachusetts Bay
the way
we once had crossed, with wine and the love

of the day. We hoisted sails before
the beach.
The reach
of land called Devils's Head passed by. The shore

of one island became the shore of the last:
Scrag, Ringtown
Gooseberry, John.
We ran before the wind as the sea passed.

Running, August 9, 1974

A summer morning,
my son and I are running the Red Point Road
for time, for the early breeze,
the half-high sun.
Elsie Gillespie is picking raspberries
by her barn-garage. She waves. Overhead
the eagle from the Sisters winds slowly higher,
pacing.
Pace will bring us home. My son
eases ahead in his long strides. There's a parked car
off the road for blueberries: summer
people. A bandana-head looks up from serious picking.

Pacing. At the turn of the woods
a crow jumps from the top of a spruce tree
caw, cawing to cronies deeper in: they
take off, protesting.
I relax into pace, unclench
my fists, try not to think of running.
My son disappears down the hill
through the Otter Pond swamp.
I love my son. I will catch him if I can.

Two miles—from the seawall field to Rosy Staples' house
and back. (We will sit on the deck, pick
berries by the shore, wade in the tide pool,
breathe easy.)
Pacing. The halfway mark, my son is coming
back. We nod. Arms loose, legs
easy, I am turning
home. Pace will bring me home. I
will not think of running. The island
is cool and green, the day is long,

my son is running like the rhyme,
if you
can, if
you can, . . .
I'm running after the gingerbread man.

The Lobsterman Off Red Point

hauls his string of summer traps, and the buoys
line the glass sea morning calm. Offshore
the whistler's ten second moan sounds another
story. Across the deck a small boy

learns addition and subtraction in Chinese. Later
he will make a drip castle on Fine Sand Beach
as the tide goes out. But now the morning's summer
eases into color and sound, teaching

the calculus of tone. Yellow jackets
prowl the railing spruce. Overhead a plane brackets
the blue sky looking for herring. You read in the sun,
your long black hair pony-tailed for fun.

The Shoals Between Red Point And The Sister

islands whiten the mid-channel
darkline:
foreground poplar coins

rattle the fog flannel
sky. Add
wild roses and the lost gold mine

near Black Point.
My view
is chartless, blue

across the water's sheen. The shoals,
fifteen feet
down, anchor point

the sailless sailboat's dream.

Mid-Tide: Families Of Black Ducks

dabble in the rockweed rising
and lowering in gentle swells:
soft

squabble across the water, emphasizing
summer calm. Below, brown bales
of kelp

unravel. When the ducks beeline
for the rainbow pots
beyond

the ledge, heart green
poplar dots
enlarge

the puzzle's theme. Nearby
you teach a small boy words
in late July.

Duck Hunting With Kaimei At The Otter Ponds

When the two Goldeneyes took off at the far end
of the first pond, they headed west,
then turned and came for the quarter moon
behind me, bright white in the late November

afternoon, rising like sixty over the blue stone
beach under my feet gunning the best
flap they could muster, already at max duck
speed, the drake flying co-pilot six feet

behind, although I confirmed that only with luck
later, after I leaped the low tide channel
to the rock island haired with kelp, and picked
him from the soft lee of the deep water side

belly up, moon white in a small funnel
cave, rising and lowering in the soft lap
of the incoming tide. There was a small
red spot on one breast and a broken

wing. When I handed him over, Kaimei
handed me back my gun. The hen
was re-crossing overhead in the first of three
passes. "Did you hear me yell?" she

asked. "I couldn't see you from the end of the beach."
We watched the hen land oceanside, beyond gun's reach.

Sister Islands Bay, Late August

Blue bay, black crow, shadow
spruce: the way the low
gliding gull settles
on the low tide meadow

(black rockweed yellowing)
wing lilting, feet first,
underscores the tolling bell
from the southwest, bellowing

faintly from Long Island Plantation
(mid-channel buoy
or Sunday summoning) in the lee
of my August imagination:

the wingstill white descent,
the un-seeming search
of the solitary perch,
the unplanned, imminent, re-ascent.

Swans Island, Mid Summer

My daughter is making bread. She kneads
the dough. For two summers she has reached
into the blue agate lobster pan, yeasty
and flour dusty, blowing the perspiration
from her upper lip. It's her business:
enriched white, breakfast bread with raisins,
onion rye. She stirs early and late,
dumping flour bags, up to her elbows in a ten
pound sog of dough, working it over, patting
it, knifing through it, plumping

it in eight pans for the oven. Little white
fat stomachs that grow grow
all in a row. I'm in the corner
reading. Grumpy. She's Snow
White, her black hair bunned, earning
her keep. The island forest broods
in the summer heat, the lobster boats
creep around the shore at half-tide
under tiny clouds of gulls. Islands

and islands, the distraction of high
summer. I lose count of my pages,
her cupsfull
of flour, her summers left.
My eyes blur. I focus on everything
that doesn't count. Reading lifts me
off the page: I remember my mother
stacking the rising loaves on the radiator
under towels, my father holding a baked

loaf in his hand, smelling it warm,
kissing the topbrown crust: the fall
of 1938 before the hurricane, a different
season before the plot thickened and I left
for good. Now I'm trying to read Theodore
Roethke: my daughter is timing
the loaves. I daydream of fishing,
I imagine I pull up another self
from the waters I sleep on
in the dark, the pile of books I lounge

over in the mid-morning sun. I think of
telling my daughter that I love her,

ooze in the half-commotion
of half-remembered loves. I would bring
a boar's heart to the queen. She
slapdabs the tile counter with an ammonia-
soaked cloth, tidies her wrapped and warm gambles
in two cardboard boxes
and heads off.

On the table is a loaf for us.

II

"The top of a sea wall is flat, about the width of a city sidewalk, and as high as the highest storm tide. The slope is gentle on the sea side, but toward the land it is very steep, resembling the wall of a fortress. The ocean has deposited its storm-gathered debris along the crest of the wall: heaps of sea-weed, stumps of trees, lengths of cordwood, sections of weirs, shattered lobster traps entangled in their rotting warps, hatches, and timbers from wrecked vessels and barges. Here and there a beach pea has taken root and nods its purple flowers at the walker, or a patch of sea lungwort lays down a carpet of mist-gray leaves. On the land side wild irises and roses bedizen the great timbers tossed over the wall by some mountainous tide of years ago."

Perry D. Westbrook, *Biography of an Island*,
Thomas Yoseloff, New York, 1958, p. 15.

Tasting Island Fruit

I part the high grass for strawberries
glinting in the sun, drawing
first blood: one tongue,

two tongues. Overhead, two gulls
squawk and wail: lookouts, summer
script: berry stems

soft in the fingers. Gull tongues
mimic our summer break, our ritual
code. Low thunderheads drift

west. Higher, rib clouds ease
east. The crows deliberate
on the rock beach. I recognize

the lobster boats winding
their tackle, circling under the gulls'
swarm, gunning

the throttlewash, blaring rock and roll,
the strains of early summer. You
are in a house reading,

weeding the lettuce, painting
an unfinished portrait:
peonies, wild

turkeys, the blackening peach-
seed on the corner of the deck,
the broken back-step

crawling with ants. *Distance*

brooks distance. I pick
through the grass to a strawberry

lair. The stems hold
on. Poplars rattle the breeze
just off the water, fair June.

Something arranges these roots
like hair. My mouth
waters, and my fingers stain.

Hauling Traps With Theodore:
a Midnight Narrative At Low Tide

The flashlight dangling from my neck
keeps dying. I am eyeing
the low places, trying
to keep upright in the wet rock-

weed. We're at the edge
of an eleven foot tide
just turning. On his side
(one foot slipping a low ledge)

my son Theodore taps the sea-
water from his light
until it flares. The night
fog silkens in the beam. He

answers "I'm OK" when I call his nick-
name through the dark
and scan my light to mark
his fall. "Thee," I call, and pick

my steps across the shell-
crushed white of the low tide
cove. "Yes," he says beside
me. My youngest son. His name tells

me what I have to know. When
I am old it will be
between us, this benediction of the foggy
cove, these periwinkle agate bells ten

times ten under our feet
as the rush of the wavelets breaks
at our knees. We make
our way to the weighted lines seated

in the crevices of the low-drain
ledges. "Here's one," Thee
says as I shuffle waist-deep toward the lee
of the inland cove. This is the Maine

coast, the summer of my
last son at home. My light blinks on,
off, on. I can see kelp flowing silky brown
through my ankles. I

reach now for the floating black
line. Thee whispers from his trap, "Two,"
as I haul. "You
better bait," I call, our voices flowing back

to back, face to face across the heavy
swells. Intimacy,
the declension of father and son, Thee
and I, second persons familiar. We

work in quiet. I lift
a keeper and a short to the clam roller, re-
bait and heave the wire trap to the sea.
A blush of bubbles, it sifts

down, gone. We haul
the other three and mount
the broadbacked ledges. We count
the summer's haul: secrets. "I'll haul

anytime, day or night," Thee
says. Inside, we take off our wet
boots and shorts, stack split
spruce in the fireplace. We

talk: now and then: fog, bait,
my father's lobster-onyx ring. In
the refrigerator produce tray, the blackening
lobsters wait.

Picking Blueberries With Uncle Harry A Month Before His Eightieth Birthday

His hands moved like ledge spiders
through the low bushes.

I talked:
"Fifteen years ago they pulped the whole
island. These slash piles
are rotten. The wood
is punky, won't burn. Good
for nothing but the ground."

He dropped blueberries
on blueberries like soft lead
balls: The best ones
are underneath the leaves."

After supper when he left the house
with a cooking pan, Howie
said, "He'd rather pick
blueberries than go fishing. I've seen
him leave Great East Lake with twelve
quarts after a weekend and give
them all away in North Berwick on his way
home."

I talked:
"These stumps are spruce. A few fir and tamarack.
The islanders call it hackmatack. The seedlings
have jumped a foot
in two years." In the twilight he slapped
one hand at mosquitoes, and picked
with the other.
"I never picked
blueberries in the dark before."

We drifted apart, picking.

In the early dark I called
to him. Thirty feet away
he said aayup without raising
his head.

My son and I crossed the road, looking
for better spots.

Later he said, "Where'd
you go, up the hill? I looked around
but I couldn't find you, so I came
home."

Ballade Of A Rowboat

hauled from the salty grass in May
where Gleason Scott up-ended it last fall
beside his duck pen. Across the bay
a southwest breeze blew up a squall
before he got it hauled and turned: "a yawl"
he said, "near Hat Island was almost blown
over and I knew she's coming all
the way." Today my son must cross alone

for the first time. It is an ordinary day
on Swans Island: the Morrison's are checking a haul
of lobsters next door at the wharf, across the way
Russell Burns is lowering our sloop at a crawl
down his boatyard track, some seagulls brawl
over bait at a lobster boat. My son skips a stone
then dips his brush in the bottom-paint all
the way. Today my son must cross alone

because he wants to do it. I hear him say
that the harbor is not far across to our sloop, a small
speck on the shore a half mile away;
we tip over the punt so the paint bottom falls
water side down and it steadies. He sits tall,
oars straight out. He waves once, his own
wave, and starts rowing. He will row all
the way. Today my son must cross alone.

I watch until he cannot hear my call
then drive my car the long way around. The tone
of his soft voice repeats, resounds: I can go all
the way. Today my son must cross alone.

Crossing By Ferry

Out in the bay the island waits, green woods
holding on, from this distance, as casually as my son
standing against the chain rail, looking at the water,
looking hard, trying to figure out something about fish
or depth, not yet sure of the question, a picture
of myself thirty-five summers ago looking into a mystery

in another part of Maine. Not a real mystery,
only a cellar hole, a family outing, the woods
around North Berwick—I can still picture
myself stepping back, my father saying come on son
see where the big house used to be. No fish
swam in that hole, but it had something to do with water.

Maybe I was scared because there wasn't any water;
anything that deep ought to be covered. My son's mystery
is his own, however. He points to a school of fish
troubling the surface fifty yards out, then the woods
on Goose Point, then Cranberry Mountain: my son,
the guide. I get my camera and take his picture.

In the background Bass Harbor Light glistens, a picture
in itself. It is four miles from us across the water,
but it seems like one. How much longer, my son asks.
Twenty minutes. The passing of time is not a mystery
to him yet. How many trees are in those woods?
I tell him more than I can count: it's like fish,

nobody knows: the water ahead is named for a fish,
Mackerel Cove. He asks if he can take a picture
of it. I agree. We pass the black gong; the woods
on shore become single trees. The tidewater
is tugging the lobster buoys and their floats—mystery
bottles hovering over the traps below. My son

asks if they had ferries when I was a son.
We watch a lobsterman pick out a large fish
from his trap and skid it along his deck, a mystery
to my son who wants to know how. I say picture
it: the bait inside the narrowing net below the water.
For the fish it's like getting lost in the woods.

As we near the shore I picture myself as my happy son,
throwing bread over the water, gulls grabbing it like fish,
mystery in his eyes, looking lovingly at the green woods.

Island Deer

in late afternoon appear
in dooryards, browsing
the high mid-summer
grass. They lift and lower

their heads, musing.

At high noon, the harbor mackerel
slash in schools
at the steel
jig, flashing.

The Mid-Summer Crows Pause On The Rockweed

and shove off, their raucous
morning caucus
now above deep spruce,
loose

as leads on a thrown net:
now set
in the dark place. Moving, they resume
their off-tune

talk onshore. In the rockweed, a mink
slinks
the morning further on, and disappears.
Here

and there a cormorant gawks and dives, his black
shadow track
now gone in the incoming tide, glistening.
I am listening.

Red Point: On the Edge of Summer

On this late morning in late June
two yellow butterflies traverse the beach peas
where the seawall begins.
Mourning doves sound in the air. I can see

Long Island Plantation, darker blue above the sun glare
sea, behind the closer Sister Island's darker green,
beyond the tide rip glaze, that intermittent creamy
mid-tide roil off Red Point's hogback shore.

We have come again to our tidal cove
of greens and blues. One poplar remains
among our shoreline spruce; its leaves
from my childhood story book flutter like coins.

Our last son at home is in China, on his way
to Shanxi to see the Buddhist shrines
color the hills. Here, a nearby birch divides like a tuning
fork before me, beyond my reach, just out of play.

Author, deck of Red Point home, Summer 2001

Early Summer Sounds

Sitting on the deck away from the mid-morning sun,
reading Mary Oliver on Whitman, I hear the bulkhead windows
of the house begin to open
downward, one by one, and I know

Kaimei is letting in the sun-fogged Sunday
morning air of this island coast. She
has returned from a long walk with the dog, and now
can hear the high tide lapping of the beach

stones as she works her way through
the preface to her teenage countryside life
in China. We have been to the Odd Fellows
Hall for breakfast with the summer clientele. My wife

and I. That rhyme in my late years seems right,
irregular but sound, akin to these deciduous larch
trees, still conifer to the bone though bare in March
before the yellow purple buds begin to form, bright

with spring: hackmatack, tamarack,
from the Montana forests above Kalispell
of my youth, to the Maine woods. Sounds tell
us more than we know: the wavelets on the rocks,

ducks softly squawking among the rockweed,
wind in the birches waving
arms across the darker spruce, the lone gull whispering
overhead, scanning the sea for her daily bread.

Island Birds

Early morning after the rain, the range
of blues and greens retains the dark night's
rainbow dream. Black cormorants in flight
from nowhere hurry singly by, and the strange

vibrato of crows lifts from the woods. I
remember little of the night except a fragment
of the long playing childhood dream, a long lost tent
opening beside a river, then closing, as if a great eye

blinked, and birches swaying in the sun
in full yellow Nod, that land of early summer play,
the way it recapitulates itself here in the early light of day
while diamond water sparkles blindingly east beneath the sun

and a lone lobster boat negotiates into the blazing light
and disappears. Yet the lingering engine hums
until the wind in the trees is the only sound, then
the crows again, nearer, slightly frenzied, still out of sight.

The Morning Calm

The intermittent sun glare from the boat hauling traps
off the Plantation shore measures the high gaps
in the cirro-cumulus clouds slowly moving east,
though the barely perceptible breeze off the water comes back west,

with its fresh morning smell. The tops of the shore spruce
are sentinel-still, fathomable only to the garrulous
crows who abide momentarily on their serious
migration deeper into the woods. Whatever truce

they reach is private, unrelated to the crosswinds
of July. I too accept the calm between,
crow-like in my own way, beneath the high easterly scene
of cotton tinged with blue and the salt cool breeze. I find

this surface scene as laden with mystery and certitude
as last night's dream where I found myself
in a turbulent land before a way home appeared. The shelf
of clouds drifts east; two dolphins cut the surface of this morning mood.

III

"World War II brought enemy submarines even into the shoal waters of nearby fishing banks where they would surface and at gun-point relieve a solitary fisherman of his catch. Depth charges trembled above the clatter of the surf. In island homes pictures fell from the walls and window panes were cracked. Squadrons of planes swept back and forth along the coast and observation blimps hovered like summer clouds above the bay. . . .

One summer morning islanders on the northern shore awoke to see the Presidential yacht at anchor a mile or two up the bay. . . . Later the only mildly surprised islanders read in the newspapers of the signing of the Atlantic Pact in the waters off Mt. Desert. Thus the streams of war flow in and out among the islands, though they haven't flooded over the shores nor lingered long in their midst."

Westbrook, p. 124-5, passim.

Summer Math On Red Point Road

I remember writing "1937" on my multiplication table
papers in Miss Reynolds' room in my yellow Lynnhurst
school, when seventy-two seemed as high as numbers were able
to reach; then weekly the twelfth numeral burst

until a hundred and forty-four seemed sufficient
for all the problems of life. Before I left that yellow school
Miss Bridgham eased me into third percentage
and the mysteries of higher math, and I was ready to travel

the bus to junior high and the world. All
my math teachers now are dead, but the calculus of memory
brings back the names as quickly as I begin to call
the roll: Misters Rice, Lahey, Watson, Haley,

and Miss Fox. They taught me more than what to count.
They taught me special days and how to give
the simple numbers meaning: how they all mount
up, one by one. Addition shows us how to live.

The First Blue, After Fog

The brush pile on the ledges before our cove
grows higher day by day, as I clear last autumn's
leveled spruce before the coming summer rain.
It looms as background to high grass before the heavy

morning fog. Even as the hidden sun arcs
higher in its morning burn, the sea remains
opaque, as if a sheet of gray has dropped behind
the quiet birches and the sleepless poplar coins. Dark

shadows in the shoreline spruce paint chiaroscuro
depths above the line where further islands yesterday
defined perspective in a different way,
with miles between, then nothing above and everything below

the surface of the Gulf of Maine. Now the first line
of random lobster buoys dots gray water as the fog
recedes, and overhead the first blue openings appear. Only time
remains before the idea of the sea is clear, even unto Spain.

Shifting Fog

The morning breakers duplicate themselves with soft rolling ease
and the sun dries the dew on the deck. The cold snap
is over, and the distant water haze
evaporates like disappearing gauze.

Only the sounds of the half-tide waves
resound with the morning calm.
We have just put down the phone
to China where our son has climbed Tai Shan.

Now the outer island fog returns.
The scraggly tops of spruce define
the Sister Island trees that curve above the cotton line.
An oil barge shadows along the bottom edge of white

and disappears across the mid-tide rip. Its engines
hum beyond Red Point and seem to stop. Again
the fog recedes, and the half-summer game goes on.
A familiar family of ducks rides the breakers like a dream.

Drying Rockweed

We have gathered rockweed from yesterday's high waves
and spread it in the sun between the poplar and the deck
to dry for our garden at home, a myriad soufflé
of yellow rubber curls, purple moss and mussels yanked

by the hair from the tide pool floor. From the deck, I
watch the tidal clock tick minor wave by wave,
whitening the basin channels. Two gulls like barrel staves
bob in the rising rockweed soup, eyeing

through water glass the rainbow bottom we have walked
within the hour. They peck and squabble over an underwater life
we cannot see. Their aim is deadly and the end foregone. Brief
summer interludes reveal the private ways we find relief.

Birch Leaves

Black seaweed laced with yellow, drapes
the boulders disappearing in the tide,
and island roses overflow the deck,
their yellow centers candy to the bees that check
each one by one. Pink blossoms ride
the wind, calming between gusts, and gape
again at the afternoon sun, as if July
could multiply the yellow summer days
of late middle age, Eden cast adrift for good,
the dead reckoning stare through the invisible hood
of days to come, as if July might simply stay.
The yellow on the birch leaves is the other story.
They sway and ruffle in the ocean breeze.
Come fall they'll droop, ready for the winter freeze.

Gray Wings In The Fog

The gull in the fog watches the tide cove fill.
The outline of his breast against the grayer white
matches the froth of the wavelets breaking into the still
scene beneath his ledge. I cannot see beyond him into the bright

mist where two lobster boats work their lines
of traps, growling buoy to buoy. Occasionally
he flaps twice to the rising rockweed at the seawall
edge and bobs among the yellow soup. When he returns

to the ledge he seems to stare beyond the scene.
When the first wave breaks across his feet he lifts again
to the gentle shoreline calm. Closer now, I can discern
his gray wings tinged with black, his yellow beak. When

he dips straight down, his patience pays off. The boats have gone.
His old ledge has disappeared. The cove is calm.

Our Morning View

The fifth day of fog breaks on our eastern shore
in the stillness of our mid-summer
stay, and a lone orange buoy floats on the edge
of white, ninety yards out from our ledge.

Our morning view is a study in onshore black and green
as the sun lifts higher above the fog. Dew glistens
on the undersides of thin birch arms
and in the tamarack fur. A passing gull returns

and banks on a dime to crash the tidal soup
where the seaweed rises from its ropey
curls and floats in yellow fronds. As diamonds bead
the rising cove, the whitest blue appears overhead.

These Roses In Mid July

overflowing on the deck
make more poignant the spruce
railings aging under the seasonal suns.
They belie their own brown
underside, their southeast bruise flecked
with twigs, and lounge in loose
array seven boards deep,
barely murmuring in the summer wind
as the summer bees flaunt
their carefree summer binge. I want
some distant day, because we cannot keep
the dearest things, to find
at least in some forgotten drawer
this barest hint of what we knew was more.

Return To Swan's Island In Late Summer

Wild roses, overlapping the edge of the deck,
have lost their blooms, and a lone bee moves in vain
from rose-hip to hip the size of peas flecked
with blush, the first traces of Maine's

second rose blossoms, sunset red, round
as giant marbles, stem-sheathed in green-fanged
Asian stars. For now, swelling without a sound,
the bush is shadow green and black. The faint clang

of the Sunken Money Ledge buoy tolls
the near-end of summer, and the near beach
peas have turned half brown. As the tide rolls
softly in, a gull swoops by, his soft screech

hanging in the air, then once again the late
summer silence of yearning, lifting again that old weight.

Fog Inventory After The August Rain

Fog webs whiten the young shore larch,
green moss stubble-beards the trunks of spruce
looming with their higher dark. Our sky-gray
tide pond merges with the mist, silently swallowing

the shadow outer ledge. When the snapping blaze
of our softwood fire turns our gaze inside, we follow
the random trail of things that clear days
overlook, when the outer view is green

islands and a tacking sail. Here's that round clay
water jug from Gredos, Spain; the wine glass from Bonn;
the yellow-blue tablecloth—St. Maries de la Mer;
the Xi'an terra cotta warrior calendar;

the round black buoy from Scotland's own east
coast. Those days come clear in the fog's white yeast.

From The Deck, The Third Day Of Fog

In the dead still silence of the low tide morning
fog, a white web reveals its interlocking frames
in knit-spun space between the green
spine ends of new growth spruce, suspension

firm, delicately twined, sky-white against the brown
late summer grass, its oblong center lace defined
by space and emanating stairs of ladder lines,
Parcheesi-like, expanding outward like a fern.

It seems to drift in air, yet holds its own
by thongs known only to its absent queen
somewhere nearby in a darker arm
of fate, waiting for the sun to warm

her woven lair. She has the time.
Nothing flies in the morning air. The fog hangs in.

Sput Staples Hauls Out In Front, Late Summer

By eight o'clock the sun is shore-spruce high
and the low tide pool mirrors the low
eastern sky, white with offshore fog.
Overhead, the cloudless onshore sky

is coloring-book blue. A lobsterman I know,
his stern sail set, hooks his toggle
buoy and wraps the trap line in the pulley
groove. His boat growls slowly in an arc

and the trap appears. I know his ritual by heart.
When he waves and disappears around the point, surely
clear days and foul will follow him home. I mark
the buoy where he has moved his trap. The black

toggle sits almost motionless on the slow
wake of the tide, six fathoms over the box below.

Sput Staples hauling traps, with passenger Yunwei Chen (1998)

After The Late August Rain

The eastern sky is dark after last night's rain
and the low cloud sun silvers the bay on a line
toward the Duck Island Light, still hidden within
the offshore storm. The morning breeze quickens

a silver change from gray to black, and the horizon
is a sudden knife of light. No human hand could mine
this scene; only the inner eye that knows the sun
in its rising. Overhead the clouds from the west

open blue gaps, and shore birches glisten
in their moist yellow-green. These island vestments
shine after the rain like some human preening.
without guile, an innocence so natural it seems

more than it is. Our August landscape
assumes a clarifying tone in its hourly changing shape.

After The Late Summer Island Visit

Soft white rollers unravel from the afternoon blue
half tide, and the sun brightens the rainbow
buoys between our inlet cove and the fog glow
of the nearer Sister shore. Thick gray glue

seals off the further view. Our childhood guests have gone.
Rollers wash our boulder beach. Soon
the sea-change begins again, as western
clouds loom overhead and the steel sea darkens

beneath the bobbing buoys. What plays out
before our eyes has all played out before,
yet it is more than a changing tidal shore.
It is the past itself and those lone buoys without

lines drifting un-retrieved on that other sea
we visit in dreams, and occasionally in our memory.

-for Roger and Lyn-

IV

"The morning after Clyde burned down his shack
With a knocked over candle—the ashes still
Too hot for us commiserators to sift through—
His nephew's backhoe rumbled up the road,
Ground to a halt, and lowered through Clyde's gaze
A vacant chickencoop creaking in its jaws."

—Robert Bagg, "Clyde Torrey." *Horsegod*,
iUniverse, 2009, 104—

Dusty Staples' buoys and traps in the Mackerel Cove fog (2010)

Lines For Kaimei During An Island Storm

The yellow hardwood fire deepens to red
coals quivering in their dying. Rain
lashes the roof, and the seaward
windows glisten where the lampshade shines,
black mirrors from the whiplash sea.
Your eight foot Chinese curtains frame the night:
silk pandas eating green and blue bamboo.
The rain-blotched windows gleam like pearls we
bargained for in Fujian, the island of Gulang-yu.
You're upstairs, downstairs, everywhere gone from sight.
This afternoon I shot a duck in the rain
and lost my hat in the wind as the tide pulled the floating
body out to sea. I watched it gain
momentum as it reached the rip between
the Sisters and Red Point, a lifeless mote.

A Cormorant Swims By Our Tide Pool, Diving

The view east through the birches is yellow-
green. Diamonds spread over the water.
As the sun lifts higher, the glitter begins to disappear.
Morning has posed its question, and the breeze tells all,
the latest news of six more boys' demise. Again
the diamonds quicken our morning
view: Long Island Plantation is a deeper green,
the waves break on the Sister's ledge, pure cream,
silent, rolling into spray, the way horizon
white beyond the further island seam
eases into tint of blue, until straight up
into this beveling morning cup.
The cormorant surfaces like memory
shuddering, stark under this military sky.

Maine High Summer: The Southwest Breeze Blows Diamonds

on the mid-morning bay and a lobster boat works the south side
of the tide rip between the western Sister and Red
Point. His toy engine is a mile away riding
the white-blue day. The constant sea change tides
him through the soft shell days of the molting gold
on the ocean floor. It is all rhythm here
and the beguiling calm of day unfolds
so orderly it draws us to the fire
at night where we remember the blaze
of stars trespassed by trails of military
convoys ferrying limb-less ageless boys
to the wards of Walter Reed in solitary
public view. On this moonless night
the planes pass over, tiny specks of light.

The Eastern Shore

Here on the headland of the old Morrison tent ground,
the fog lifts and re-gathers under an old summer sky.
I can make out the top third of a stern sail
inching toward the cut beyond Black Point
and the line of metal gray where the channel tide
colors the breathless morning calm of that old June
when Clyde Torrey's farm was up on higher ground
and his horse Sandy grazed the nearby field beneath a sky
so cerulean blue that a summer artist painting sails
changed from watercolor to oils. This foreground point
quickens days with clover and buttercups and tides
that give and take away this rocky beach and June
itself. The bone yard airport on the headland rise is gone;
Mertic too, and Gleason, even Bud. Ground is home.

Near The Ferry Landing, Mid-Summer

An empty rowboat rocks on anchor at noon
in Mackerel Cove. White caps roil under the sun.
The little boat snarls at the anchor line
in its mouth, unaware of the quarry stone
below. Green is black under the noon sun,
spruce lines to the Carrying Place where Indians
once crossed, canoeing to Isle of Haut. Now no one
in sight as the summer white caps flash through the noon
hour, and the little boat rocks. A new Ford Fairlane
with a lone driver appears on the ferry road, turns
around and drives back again. Once upon a time,
Richard Kent's floating lobster car deepened
this view toward Island Retreat where the clam
flats come and go. That too is gone.

From The Lighthouse As The Fog Comes In

The plaintive cry of a lone gull
cuts the gathering fog, and the channel bell
rocks its toll. Early summer gives and takes
away. The tops of Harbor Island's spruce
go white, and Normie Burns heads out. His wake
disappears under the folds of seamless sheets.
The cedar top of this boarded-up house
is graying white. Another lone gull bleats
his cry and lands on the peak of the roof.
The only sound is an invisible boat, faint
near an invisible shore. The only proof
that color exists is the near grass and the taint
of spirea in the mist. Again the sound of the knell
below, the invisible rocking of the channel bell.

At The Draining Of The Quarry Pond

The late July fog hangs outside the bell
in Burnt Coat Harbor, and the lighthouse
disappears and forms again. From the north rim
of the stone quarry, the brown surface of the draining
pond clears to overhead blues. Workmen douse
the geometric slabs of the lowering wall,
blackened in the murk for a hundred years.
Their small barge noses against the granite bier,
the gas generator grumbling through the noon hour.
When the water came in, the springs spurted so strong,
four men drowned at the bottom. The gong
near the lighthouse still tolls their deaths. Now gulls
cruise and circle the massive granite shell.
Someone has thrown a white lobster buoy in the well.

Minturn: The View Across To Burntcoat Harbor Light

Looking across to the Western Way this cold
July noon in the nursery school parking
lot, the bell buoy spots the channel, stark
on the steel harbor lake, tide-pulled
in its distant western lean, dark spruce bold
in black-green channel cliff descent.
A white line trails a lobster boat, its distant
wake now thin. White daisies lean and hold
their own in this foreground scene. All this I see
I will take with me while we are absent
one from the other, and all our words in recent
skirmishes will fade like thorns in the memory
of roses blooming over the deck. They blaze
in fog and sun. Bees nuzzle in their summer craze.

Looking Across Mackerel Cove Into The Summer Fog

The small tidal cove beyond Dusty Staples' wharf
tints foreground green, then white. Out there four miles
in the white, Blue Hill names the bay. While
the tide recedes, the morning is cut in half
by four noisy crows across the street: three-toned,
they alternate between hysterical
and calm, then vanish, only to return more vocal,
more aggrieved. All the summer news is local.
When the store burned down, it was sensational.
Now the summer fog is white as bone.
Dusty's buoys snug in fives on the wharf,
red and white, great coils of line, piled traps at half
tide. When the crows are gone the tidal weed
appears. Daisy centers glow in the fog like beads.

Swan's Island: The Third Summer of the Iraq War

Where the tide rips between the nearest Sister
and Red Point on the eastern shore, the fog rolls in
in late afternoon, and the gulls and the crows begin
their half-tide watch. High summer consists
of such low key natural shenanigans
where the sun increases the black in the shore spruce
and yellows the poplar green. Everything is close;
fog does the trick. The lobster buoys are gone
into the white. Once, twenty-three
years ago, a whale swam by, so long
that part of her was submerged. We were so young,
in retrospect, we ran to the shore in glee
and watched her rise straight up, where we saw
thousands of herring gushing down the sides of her maw.

Late Morning At The Water Lily Pond

Two little girls wearing bike helmets
pick duck feathers from the shore
wishing they could take a boat "out there,"
then disappear down the road, leaving the jet
black hooded ducks, now curious, to me
at the newly calm edge of the water-lillies,
tucking their heads against their wings to form
an uneven line of brown drowsers among the green
pads shining and curling in the August wind.
Bob Tozier lived across the street, but he's gone.
Beyond the field, Agnes Staples is no longer home.
Mrs. (doughnuts) Higgins also left this view behind.
These white lilies, undisturbed in their basking,
give all their fragrance just for the asking.

Toothacher Cove On The Old Abbott Road

The yellow mid-tide weed beyond the beach
wavers in the August broth beneath
the fog, masking the tidal shore in the late
summer calm, almost the color of the chestnut
leaves now curling on Atlantic lawns in an island
peace that gives and takes away the far away
view in a minute's time. Even now the reach
of the fog withdraws and I can see the half-wreath
of green-yellow grass where the Carrying Place gateway
beckoned Indian voyagers to Isle of Haut.
A family with a yellow float plays in the sand.
A sloop with a yellow punt defines the gray
offshore. Driving home I'll pass the yellow
ribbons that beckon us again toward the fall.

Crows In Fog

Ah, summer at the languid shore in Maine—
the whisper tremble of our tidal cove
in fog as crows drop down in silence, one
by one from sentinel shore-lined dark spruce alcoves
in the shadow mist. From our window
view we cannot see them in the smoothened
seawall beach stones sloping toward the low
tide morning hush where patchy white gauze curtains
drift and disappear. Invisibly,
they pock the tidal beach stone cobbled field.
The only sound is our sulky fire's punky
snapping spruce. Then a raucous blacksheen guild
explodes through live spruce into our white birch woods
and a seawall stranger looms, un-pursued.

The End Of August At Dead Man's Beach

The late morning sun blackens the spread
of buoys dotting this southern view from the red
slopes of elephant-back granite beds
enclosing Dead Man's Beach. The ocean is a lake.
Half the beach is white watermelon boulders that bake
in the sun before the spruce; half, lesser roundheads
of grayer hue above the miniature
cove of darker blue between. Late summer
is all about color and calm. When the *Lunette Christine*
circles to its pot before me just off shore,
forty pristine gulls circle and pine
for their supper at noon, the eternal encore
of the sea, these sounds like weeping sirens
before a long lost beach on a forgotten shore.

Giacometti At The Tide Pool

We emerge after sunrise to see the shadow heron
printed below her scalpel gaze, framed
by our poplar and the peeled spruce rail here on
the island shore. All else is stilled by her brazen
stare, fixing us and the pool below
and when we slowly open the camera-eye door
she wafts bay-ward, silently in soft slow
elegant downsweep flight. Now as before,
when we slept, the shore is mock serene
with semi-precious daybreak colors: cooked
egg white of the nosey circling gulls, their hooked
beaks open with their eerie moans, and one
black cormorant streaming southwest. The heron print
stays with us through the day as the sea grinds
and birches flutter behind the tall spruce blinds.

James Gillespie, (Minesweeper YMS 82; Submarine USS Balao, 1942-1945)

Down on the blue beach after four days of fog,
the afternoon half tide ruffles at its edge
and froths. A low stone wall seems a lichen hedge
before the vacant house; broken toggle
buoys and tumbled traps color the stone
beach. Our neighbor Jim is dying now
as the tide goes out, and a distant sloop with its bowsprit
vacant, edges toward Long Island Plantation.
Smooth blue stones descend in layers to the new
wavelets at the shore, and spotless gulls
stand vigil on the half-tide shoal. Wind pulls
a sail, they say, when it blows. If that is true
an offshore breeze could pull a regatta through
this island passage, now blue and darker blue.

The Late Summer Cove

Reflecting, after the storm, on the diamond surface
of Red Point cove, I hear a distant chain
saw whine and die. The wind dies too. The sheen
of tiny mackerel scales, cosmic lace,
traces half across my morning view. Emily
called it "the errand of the eye out on
the bay." First come, last eye, the memory
of last night's sky at the wharf, the passing storm,
and now this view, the white birch canopy,
these cut stone glimpses of a summer cove.
My errand stakes me to a similar grove
beyond this summer bay, that panoply
of diamond blue where a similar silence deigns
to drop things into place, and stone remains.

Rose Hips Over The Deck

The leaves of my yew-birch begin to brown
in the late summer sun. It is high tide
on the Saturday before Labor Day, and my tan
rose stars grow hips on the shore side
of the deck. Across the blue water a gull
heads north, a cormorant south. The high water
froths at the shore. Thoreau's comment on world
news weighs heavy in the clear air as crows jaw
in dark spruces behind our road. Come
October, these hips will be blood red. I move
to the ledges to keep pace with the setting sun.
Here, I am just above the tide easing on our cove
with its late summer wash. The waves keep time
by moonspeed gathering in the silent rhyme.

Early Autumn View

Looking east in September at low tide,
the island passage is rare stone bright
as the wind ruffles the morning blue.
All that moves in this early calm will soon
beguile another eye: this poplar light
of rippling coins, this squirrel, red on the side
I cannot see as I face the sun. He too
deliberates his next step on the run
in our shared domain. He is a study in wary
moves as reflections shift with the sun's arc.
Now straight across to Long Island Plantation, faery
sparkles spread across the reach toward the dark
woods angling up from the Red Point ledge.
The autumn green is darker than the deepest hedge.

September Sunday Morning At Goose Pond

Here on the west shore where the breeze ruffles
the lily pads, my view through the maple leaves
dots the blue sky red. All sounds are muffled
except the occasional wind in the onshore trees.
Dead trunks lean across my picture view
and the pond is mine, all the golden hearts
of lilies white with silken spears in the blue
mirrors between the skirt-split pads. Parts
of my childhood drift across the gently troubled
pond, four wars ago. These white pond
lilies bring it back, coiled in double
wrap inside my mother's shallow round
dish. I can hear the distant bell of the Baptist
church, and so gauge the bend in a gnarled white birch.

The Birthday Cake:
Remembering Clyde Torrey on Swan's Island

Clyde Torrey with his horse Sandy: mid-seventies before the farm fire

The birthday cake was four and a half months old when I saw it for the first time. Clyde kept it on top of the unused stove in the part of the house that used to be the kitchen. He put it there so his cats couldn't get at it. When I arrived on the island at the end of June he had flailed both arms and grinned as I pulled into the dirt and clamshell driveway. We had been friends for five years. At the post office Ethel Staples told me that he had a bad shock during the winter and couldn't talk right.

As I got out of the car Clyde was hopping toward me. On the hop he scooped up a small black kitten in one hand and kicked a rooster out of the way without breaking stride. He held up the kitten and said, "Jackie Kennedy" the way my year and a half old daughter had pronounced her first word: "KEN-NA-DY!" Except for several goddams they were among the few words I clearly understood that day. As Clyde laughed I could see that his two nicotine-stained lower teeth were still in cigar-chewing condition. I said, "You've got some more kittens, Clyde."

He made a grunting sound in the back of his throat that meant yes, said something that resembled "c'mon. . . c'mon" and motioned for me to follow him into the house.

At one time the farmhouse must have been a beauty. Several acres of fields sloped toward the ocean on the east side, and on a clear day Placentia and Black islands seemed a few hundred yards offshore. In fact they were a mile away, directly east. To the north one could see Mt. Cadillac and Mt. Champlain on Mt. Desert Island across Blue Hill Bay. One could spot the ferry as it moved several times a day between Mackerel Cove and Bass Harbor on Mt. Desert Island.

I followed Clyde over the back step which had settled into the doorway grass and entered the dark room. The smell of cats and kerosene told me that everything was the same as last year. Clyde led me directly to the stove and pointed to the cake. The stove was covered with old cigar boxes bulging with letters, and empty coffee and chicken cans full of small bottles. I knew that Clyde kept his paregoric in the small bottles.

Clyde pointed to the cake and nodded for me to read the frosting inscription. As I read he grinned and made a sound of satisfaction in his throat that meant "now THERE" but came out like "uh." I could see that he had been nipping on one of his paregoric bottles because a thin line of thick white drool was easing over his bottom lip into his chin whiskers.

The cake looked like a small caved-in ivory fortress. The sides were slanted in and the middle was slightly sunken. It looked two or three weeks old. The inscription in faded yellow and red lines of hardened sugar said "To Clyde on his 75th." Sticking out from underneath the cake was a torn piece of cardboard on which Clyde had printed with a ball point pen, "from niece Etta." Scotch-taped to the side of the stove underneath the cake was another torn piece of cardboard on which Clyde had printed "one pack of Dexter cigars and a generous drink happy birthday Clyde from Spencer and the boys."

I said, "It's a beautiful cake, Clyde.

Clyde said "uh" and launched into a lyrical and spirited explanation of his birthday celebration. His voice rose and fell with gusto and I could understand just enough to tell that it had been a mighty fine moment. As he talked he reminded himself of something else and began to search through the old cigar boxes for a letter. He was immediately agitated and said "goddam" several times. Because of the rising and falling of his voice I was able to get, "Now where did I put that goddam thing?" He went through three boxes without success, batted a cat off the stove, and turned to a table against the blackened window with more cigar boxes on it.

I said, "You got a letter, Clyde."

He said "uh" and rifled through two more boxes.

I said, "Who's it from, Clyde?"

Without lifting his head he said with exasperation something like "ob early. . . ob early. . . OB EARLY!" He had obviously said it a few minutes earlier but I hadn't understood and Clyde was irritated that he hadn't been able to make himself understood.

"GODDAM IT," he thundered and stalked into the old pantry. He opened a floor cupboard and shined his flashlight inside.

"Aah," he said, and lifted the letter off a dirty tin plate. He handed it to me and said, "uh."

I said, "Oh, it's from Bob Burly."

Clyde said "uh" with complete satisfaction. Clyde grinned as I read the letter. It expressed dismay over Clyde's shock and good wishes for a speedy recovery.

I said, "Gee Clyde that's a really nice letter. I hope Bob'll be here again this summer." Bob Burly was Clyde's best friend among the summer people. Bob and his wife regularly come to the island for two weeks in July and pitch their tent on the island tent ground owned by Clyde's nephew, Mertic.

Clyde's farm is also on the tent ground, and Mertic wants to tear down the house and put Clyde in a comfortable trailer home but Clyde says that he was born in that house and is going to die in that house. Bob Burly spends most of his vacations fixing one of Clyde's several abandoned cars on the farm for Clyde to use as spare parts to keep one of them going. The previous summer Clyde had told my wife that Bob Burly was his right arm and I was his "right bowel." It was a compliment straight out of the *New Testament*.

Clyde said "uh" and laughed a long hearty laugh. He became serious and motioned for me to follow him past the stove into the room where he lived. Years before it had been the front room of the house. Some of the window panes were broken and Clyde had stuffed rags into the smaller holes. Other panes were boarded up from the inside. The room was darker than the kitchen and the smell of cats and kerosene was heavier. The small couch on the left was littered with cats. Other cats on the floor were eating from tin pie plates crusted with government powdered milk and powdered eggs. One cat was sitting on a table that formerly had been a writing desk. The cat had one eye and one ear and an open sore on the top of his head. Clyde swept it off the table with one motion of his open palm and began another search through several old tins.

Three cans half-full of steaming liquid were heating on top of one of the two kerosene stoves. Clyde kept coffee hot during the day. Beside the stove was a case of Atlantic gelatin. He had explained to me before about the gelatin. Clyde puts raw gelatin in his coffee for his ulcer. He believes that gelatin is full of natural protein.

Clyde said "aah" and lifted a six ounce bottle of paregoric out of an old empty government whole-chicken can. He held it up to me to see and launched into a long explanation of how he came by it. I missed most of it but got "octa."

I said, "Your doctor sent it to you."

He said "uh" and laughed. He uncapped the bottle and poured about a teaspoonful into one of the cans of hot coffee and gelatin on the stove and took several gulps of the coffee. Some of it drizzled down the right side of his mouth as he drank and I could see that part of his mouth was still paralyzed. At the post office Ethel Staples had told me that after the shock he couldn't walk or do anything. She said, "It's the old car he lives in during the winter. It'll kill him."

Everyone knows that Clyde moves into one of his old cars during the coldest part of the winter. For years the islanders have talked about it. Clyde removed the back seat from an old Pontiac and installed a kerosene stove. The car is the only place he can keep warm. The house is as porous as a sieve. Clyde listens to the radio several hours a day and his only radio is in the car. He alternates several batteries as they run down from radio use. Clyde takes the dead batteries to the tent ground wash house where he keeps a battery charger plugged in to the outside electrical outlet. Day and night, one of Clyde's batteries hums beside the charger. Clyde's nephew Mertic never mentions the electricity bill.

I said, "How's your garden, Clyde?"

"Marvelous!" he said, as clearly intoned as the opening of Beethoven's Fifth symphony. I couldn't figure out why some words came out clearly and others garbled, and I followed him into the kitchen where he pointed through the grimy window to the field where he had planted potatoes, string beans, butternut squash and "greens."

Clyde is famous for his potatoes. He always plants red ones, white ones, and blue ones. He calls them his patriotic potatoes. One of the down east magazines carried a story about them a few years back. The red potatoes are Harmony Beauties, the blue ones are Nova Scotia Blues. Many years ago Clyde was featured in Ripley's "Believe It or Not" as the man who ploughed his fields with an ox and a cow yoked together.

Clyde pointed to his freshly ploughed field and ejaculated words furiously. I heard "goddam" several times and thought that he was talking about the deer that nibbled the green shoots as they appeared in his garden. I could see poles stuck in the ground with old hub caps dangling from them by wires. I could also see parts of old wagons around the edges of the newly turned sod. I said "You're worried about the deer, Clyde."

"no. . .. no. . . NO!" he said and started again. I understood the words "car" and "brother Sheldon" and figured out that he had hitched his plough by chains to the back of his car and had ploughed the field with his car. Several times the rear axle had disappeared into the fresh soil and Mertic had to pull him out with a bulldozer.

I said, "You ploughed your field with a car, Clyde."

"Aah" he said and laughed and laughed. It was clearly a triumph of the mechanized world over nature. Clyde's horse Sandy had died of pneumonia the previous fall and everyone on the island had wondered what would happen to Clyde's garden. Years ago many of the island farms had gardens but when the lobster business boomed in the forties the gardens disappeared.

I said, "I have to go, Clyde. I want to see how Gleason is coming on my house."

Clyde nodded and hummed his assent as if it was a perfectly reasonable statement. We walked out into the yard. Coming through the doorway Clyde picked up a white and black kitten and petted it. He held it up to me and laughed and said, "Nero." He tickled Nero under the chin and laughed again.

I said, "I'll be back soon. I'm here for a whole year, you know."

Clyde nodded and laughed. As I drove off I saw him pick up another kitten, take a kick at a hen walking in front of him, and disappear into the house.

During the summer, fall, and winter, I visited Clyde about once a month. Each time his speech was improved and I could understand more of what he said. Each time he beckoned me into the house and I saw the cake on top of the stove. Between visits I thought about the cake and anticipated its condition. I expected it to look more dismal as the months passed, but except for its slightly darkening hue caused by the kerosene fumes it always looked relatively the same. The candles stabilized at 45° angles. The concave sides took on the proportions of ancient rounded shoulders. The cake looked like a table model of an abandoned prehistoric city.

After the first few visits the cake seemed to be as much a part of the house as Clyde himself. The passage of days made no difference. Instead of disintegrating, the cake seemed to become more confident of its cakeness. It took on the properties of a stalagmite risen from the top of the unused stove. No longer a transient cake, it became an eternal cake. Neither cats nor friends nor storm of night could budge the cake from the top of the stove. Clyde went about his business. He fed the cats and cultivated his garden.

By mid-summer I realized that Clyde's attitude toward the cake was the crucial factor in the cake's destiny. Clyde expected it to stay the same. He took the cake's presence for granted. He also remembered to whomever he showed the cake. After he showed it to someone, he never mentioned it to that person again, but he continued to show it to newcomers and old friends who had not yet celebrated his 75th with him. I too began to take the cake for granted. During the summer and early fall I forgot about it.

When I visited Clyde in August he gave me a pail of small round potatoes and a butternut squash. He could have given me larger potatoes but he knew that the small ones are better to boil and eat with the skins on. The pail was ripped down the side and had a hole in the bottom that Clyde covered with a piece of cardboard. The pail was totally battered but he made it clear that he wanted it back. I thought to myself, "It's an eternal pail."

In September I brought a friend to visit Clyde. It was eleven o'clock on a Sunday night and my friend was leaving on the early ferry the following morning. He too had known Clyde for several years and wanted to have a goodbye drink with him. Clyde had already shown him the cake.

There was no light inside the house as we drove in the driveway and we found Clyde out back, asleep in the front seat of his car. The radio was on. Clyde had fallen asleep listening to the Red Sox baseball game from Boston. As we approached the car I called, "Hey Clyde!"

He immediately lifted his head and began to get out of the car. He said something that sounded like, "I wasn't asleep."

I said, "Bill's going in the morning and we brought some vodka. We thought you'd have a drink with us."

Clyde said, "I gunda yes" and started into the house. "By Thunder" was one of his favorite expressions, along with "By the Gods of War" and "By Chowder." During a visit he would use at least one of these expressions. Except for "goddam" he rarely swore—only when he was most upset. He never used four letter words. The angriest I ever saw him was the day his brother Sheldon was on his roof trying to follow Clyde's instructions in nailing on a strip of tarpaper with pine slabs. Sheldon wasn't getting it just right and Clyde got so upset that he stamped his feet and bellowed. He wasn't excoriating his brother, he was addressing the universe, pouring out the accumulated grievances of the years. He stamped his feet and roared "ASSHOLE" again and again.

Clyde came out of the house that night with his accordion. A tam-o'-shanter was cocked on one side of his head. In his younger days he traveled the eastern Maine coast and played at dances. He doesn't hit all the notes anymore but he gets the gist of it, and he held his head back and opened his mouth and sang as he pulled the accordian open and shoved it together again. He loves to play the accordion but he gets it out only two or three times a year, always during the summer and fall. It is the highest occasion he can muster.

Bill poured the vodka into paper cups we had brought. Clyde drank his down, wiped his hand across his wet whiskers, and roared through "Love Lifted Me." He missed several notes in the chorus and said something like "I'm not missing those notes, the keyboard's stuck."

It was a warm starry night and we stood in back of Clyde's house drinking vodka and singing. We could see the lights across the bay on Mt. Desert Island. We went through "Let the Lower Lights be Burning" and "Amazing Grace" and "Home on the Range." We saw the small light of a high jet plane moving far across the edge of the night sky. It seemed a universe away. We finished the vodka and sang "Peg of My Heart" and "The Old Rugged Cross."

When we told Clyde it was time for us to go he played the first few bars of "Auld Lang Syne" and looked at us to see if it was all right. Clyde never detains anybody longer than they want to stay and he wanted to make sure. We immediately started to sing and Clyde grinned and closed his eyes and tilted his head back as if he could see beyond the heavens and we sang "For Auld Lang Syne." The tears came to my eyes and I glanced at Bill. His were misty. When we concluded with the last words, ". . .yours and mine," Clyde lowered his head and nodded. His eyes were clear and he was grinning.

I visited Clyde at Thanksgiving and he gave me two cusks. Sonny Sprague had brought him three cusks he had caught in one of his lobster traps, and Clyde knew that he couldn't get through more than one before the other two spoiled. As he led me past the stove into his pantry I glanced at the cake. It looked about three weeks old. I thought, "It must be petrified."

Just before Christmas, Clyde drove his car down the dirt road to our house on the Red Point shore. It was early evening, and raining. Clyde wasn't supposed to drive on the town roads because his license had been revoked several years before when he went off the road and the registry people on the mainland thought him a menace. The islanders knew different but nobody could do anything about it. Clyde came through the door holding a five gallon lobster bucket. He was dripping wet. Inside the bucket was a freshly decapitated rooster. The white, yellow, and black tail feathers were matted together with rain. The breast feathers were shiny with fresh blood. I said, "Take off your coat, Clyde, and sit in front of the fire."

He said "Good" and leaned backwards into a chair. With both hands he lifted one leg out to one side and rubbed it and leaned back again. He said "Lame." His clothes smelled heavily of kerosene. I knew that Clyde wanted something.

If Clyde wanted something he would always give you something first. He would either bring you a gift or wave your car to a stop as you drove past his house. Such gifts were different than the ordinary gifts he might present you when you dropped in for a visit. He would never ask for what he wanted until you asked him if he needed anything.

I said, "You've got a lame leg, Clyde. You've been working too hard."

He said that his goddamed roof leaked. I knew that if he had been up on his roof this time of year he must be living in the house this winter instead of in the car. I said, "You're getting your house tight for winter, Clyde."

He began a long explanation of his move from the car to the house. His nephew had given him an ultimatum. I understood just enough to realize that his feelings had been hurt. He began to cry. He sobbed like a small boy. Then he shook his head as if to clear it and changed the subject.

I said, "This is your first visit to our new house, Clyde."

Clyde jumped out of his chair and did a little hop of celebration around the room. A little stream of white drool was leaking into his whiskers and I knew he had been into the paregoric. Clyde sang a brief song that I couldn't understand, and said something about his initiating the new pine floor. He nodded approval when I offered him some bourbon, and sat down and rubbed his lame leg. When I handed him the half glass of bourbon and water he drank it in several gulps connected together by heavy breathing through his nose.

Then Clyde became serious and described how he had once lost a boat on Red Point. It was a torrential night and the sea was mountainous. Clyde said that the Lord apparently hadn't wanted him that night because He passed up an easy chance. It was a northeast gale. Clyde had made the run between Black Point and Placentia Island on the east side of Ram Island, and couldn't make it through the tide rip between the south point of the western Sister and Red Point.

He pronounced "Placentia" as "Pla-centsh." When the boat hit the ledge, Clyde leaped onto the huge rock and walked to Lester Staples' house and made a phone call. He was proudest of the fact that with one call he summoned fifty men and three tackles to Red Point in thirty minutes. He shouted, "FIFTY MEN AND THREE

TACKLES." He pronounced it "TAKE-ELS." I asked him if he salvaged the boat, but Clyde shook his head in the negative and shouted, "FIFTY MEN AND THREE TAKE-ELS!"

I said, "The men must have thought a lot of you, Clyde" and he nodded approval, as if yes, that was the point. He sat back, satisfied that I had perceived the real point of the story.

I asked him if he needed anything and he said that if I had any to spare, he could use a few roofing nails. I gave him five pounds of roofing nails in a paper bag that he put in his lobster bucket. Before he left he told us to bail the gravy to the rooster.

I drove past Clyde's house daily on my way to the post office in Atlantic, and often saw him puttering outside. Clyde had long since "brushed" his house with fresh spruce and fir branches snugged against the foundation, but he continued through the cold months to hammer nails through clapboards and add board stripping to windows and doors.

In mid-February I stopped to visit. The temperature was 5° above zero. I pushed open the back door of Clyde's house, entered the old kitchen, and pushed the door closed behind me. I stood still for a minute while my eyes adjusted to the darkness. As I stepped toward the door leading to the front room where he lived, I glanced at the stove expecting to see the birthday cake. It was gone. For a split second I wondered if Clyde was still alive.

I took one step toward the door leading to the front room and could hear a radio. I banged on the door with my gloved hand and yelled, "Clyde!"

He called out for me to wait a minute. Presently he pulled the door open from the inside by a rope that he had inserted where the door knob had been. He shined a flashlight in my face.

I said, "I stopped by to see how you're doing."

Clyde was excited. He said "Finest kind. . . finest kind" and beckoned. He had something to show me. I stepped into the room and pushed the door closed. Someone had given him a radio that he turned off. He pointed to a cardboard box dangling from a wire strung across the room, and proceeded to try to unhook it.

Both kerosene stoves were lit and the room was comfortably warm. At least fifteen cats had adjusted themselves in various dozing and eating positions. The gelatin coffee was steaming on one of the stoves. One pane of one window had been almost wiped clean and the winter sun streamed through and lighted a small square on the far wall.

Clyde pulled over a chair and stood on it underneath the cardboard box. He was laughing and jabbering in the back of his throat. When he talked fast I still couldn't understand him, but when he relaxed I could get almost all of what he said. I could still understand "GODDAM" which he had said two or three times.

The box was wrapped with wire and connected to the ceiling wire by a U-bolt with an eight penny nail pushed through the openings. Clyde couldn't see over his head without his flashlight so I picked it up and shined it on the U-bolt. When he could see what he was doing he calmed down and explained that he had put the box there so the cats couldn't get at it.

I said, "You got something in the mail, Clyde."

Clyde said no, "GODDAMMIT IT TO HELL" and pulled the nail out from the U-bolt. I caught the box in both hands as it dropped.

"Open it. . . open it," he said.

As I folded open the cardboard flaps Clyde began to laugh. He shined the flashlight inside the box. It was a fresh birthday cake, frosted white with yellow sugar letters pushed gently into the frosting. The letters spelled, "HAPPY BIRTHDAY CLYDE ON YOUR 76th." Clyde laughed and laughed.

I said, "I didn't know it was your birthday, Clyde. Happy birthday."

Clyde said "Yesterday" and looked at the cake as if it was gold bullion. He wanted me to read the card. Clyde had written in pencil on the envelope, "from niece Etta." I congratulated him again and we folded the box tight and strung it to the ceiling wire with the U-bolt and the nail. I realized then that last year's cake must have been four and a half months old when I saw it last June.

Driving home I thought of the cake in the cardboard box, dangling over the communal lives of Clyde and the cats in their winter room on the west side of the ramshackle house. The birthday cake was above it all. Clyde fed the cats and cursed them and loved them. The cats completed their sides of the bargain by being present for the eating and cursing and loving.

The birthday cake, however, was not for eating. Like Clyde it had an existence of its own. It would be displayed and admired and fussed over. It would survive the winter and summer and fall. It would be impregnable as long as necessary. When the year was over it would be replaced.

I don't know what Clyde did with the cake of his 75th birthday. I'm sure that he disposed of it in his own way in a moment of high privacy. I'm sure that he let it go as he let the years go from his life. Other years and other cakes lie ahead.

Last week when I drove past Clyde's house he was lying on a ladder held fast to his roof by a rope that stretched up and over the peak of the house and tied to an old apple tree in the yard. His brother Sheldon was standing beneath him on another ladder leaning against the house. Clyde was hammering oak laths over a newly-placed strip of tarpaper. I thought of the birthday cake dangling from the inside ceiling somewhere beneath Clyde.

When the warm weather comes, Clyde will take the cake out of the cardboard box and put it on top of the unused stove. By late spring the ivory frosting will be dusted with kerosene fumes and the candles will begin imperceptibly to slant inside the dark old kitchen. Even now I can see the cake in my mind's eye.

Clyde died a few months after the old farmhouse burned down one summer in the late seventies, and I wrote this memoir of him shortly afterward. I have kept it with affection similar to his own sentiments pertaining to the birthday cakes of his later years, but unlike Clyde, I have never shared it with others until now. DJ